IN A TREE

David M. Schwartz *is an award-winning author of children's books, on a wide variety of topics, loved by children around the world.* Dwight Kuhn's *scientific expertise and artful eye work together with the camera to capture the awesome wonder of the natural world.*

For a free color catalog describing Gareth Stevens Publishing's list of high-quality books and multimedia programs, call 1-800-542-2595 (USA) or 1-800-461-9120 (Canada). Gareth Stevens Publishing's Fax: (414) 225-0377.

Library of Congress Cataloging-in-Publication Data

Schwartz, David M.
    In a tree / by David M. Schwartz; photographs by Dwight Kuhn.
        p. cm. — (Look once, look again)
    Includes bibliographical references (p. 23) and index.
    Summary: Introduces, in simple text and photographs, the characteristics of
some of the trees and animals that can be found in a forest. Includes a caterpillar,
raccoon, yellow warbler, owl, squirrel, a white pine, and an oak.
    ISBN 0-8368-2245-5 (lib. bdg.)
    1. Forest animals—Juvenile literature. 2. Trees—Juvenile literature.
3. Animals—Juvenile literature. [1. Forest animals. 2. Trees.]
I. Kuhn, Dwight, ill. II. Title. III. Series: Schwartz, David M.
Look once, look again.
QL112.S39 1998
590—dc21   98-6308

This North American edition first published in 1999 by
Gareth Stevens Publishing
1555 North RiverCenter Drive, Suite 201
Milwaukee, Wisconsin 53212 USA

First published in the United States in 1997 by Creative Teaching Press, Inc., P.O. Box 6017, Cypress, California, 90630-0017.

Text © 1997 by David M. Schwartz; photographs © 1997 by Dwight Kuhn. Additional end matter © 1999 by Gareth Stevens, Inc.

Printed in the United States of America

1 2 3 4 5 6 7 8 9 03 02 01 00 99

IN A TREE

by David M. Schwartz

photographs by Dwight Kuhn

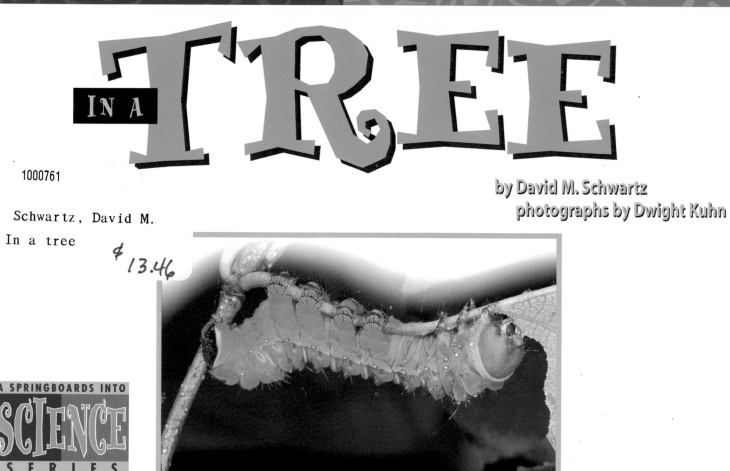

Gareth Stevens Publishing

MILWAUKEE

This paw is made for climbing trees and for holding seeds and nuts.

5

Red squirrels climb tall trees with the help of their long nails. They also collect fruit and nuts with their paws. Acorns are a favorite food.

Squirrels do not eat all of their food right away. They hide some for another day. Sometimes they cannot find all the acorns they have hidden. Those acorns may grow into oak trees.

Whoooooooo has such big, wide eyes that help it see in the dark?

An owl, that's whoooooooo!
The owl takes off on soft, silent wings.
Its big eyes help it see at night.
It will pounce on a mouse
and grab it with its
powerful feet.

VALLEY PARK
ELEMENTARY LIBRARY

Up close, they look like giant green sticks, but they are as thin as needles.

9

They are the needles of a pine tree. Some trees, like this white pine, have long, narrow leaves called needles.

Some trees drop all their leaves in autumn. Most trees with needles do not lose their leaves all at once. They are called evergreens.

What rascal wears a black mask across its face?

11

It is a raccoon. Raccoons are clever and curious. They are always trick-or-treating! If they cannot find treats, they try a trick, like turning over garbage cans at night. When they have had enough to eat, they may curl up and go to sleep in a hollow tree.

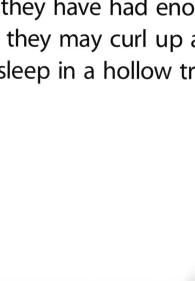

Up close, it looks like green and yellow candy.
It is not food for people — but it is for birds!

A caterpillar has six legs on the front of its body. It also has fleshy stumps called prolegs that grip twigs. Soon, this caterpillar will become a luna moth. It will no longer have prolegs — but big, beautiful, green wings.

Is this a mess that someone should clean up?
Or is it there for a reason?

A yellow warbler builds its nest in the fork of a tree. The small bird collects grasses and the silky fibers of plants. Then it weaves them into a sturdy cup and lines the nest with fine grass and soft hair. Soon, the bird will lay eggs in the nest.

Is this a colorful painting? Or is it something that falls in autumn?

LOOK AGAIN

In autumn, many leaves change color. Green leaves turn red, yellow, orange, brown, or purple.

Where do all the colors come from? They were in the leaves all summer, but green pigment covered them. In autumn months, the green disappears to reveal the many colors. The leaves are very beautiful, but soon they will fall to the ground.

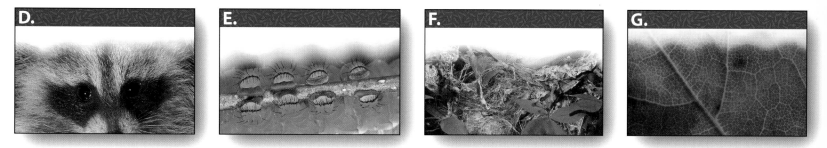

Look closely. Can you name these plants and animals?

LOOK AGAIN

A. Red squirrel

B. Owl

C. White pine

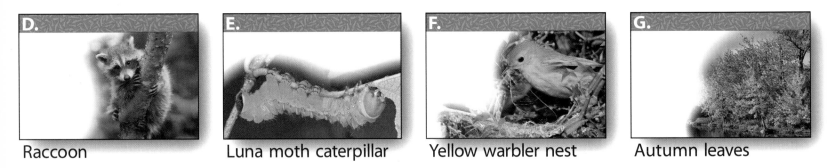

D. Raccoon

E. Luna moth caterpillar

F. Yellow warbler nest

G. Autumn leaves

How many were you able to identify correctly?

acorn: the nut of an oak tree. Birds and other animals eat acorns.

caterpillar: the wormlike larva of a moth or butterfly.

curious: eager to find out about something.

evergreen: a tree or plant that stays green all year long. Pine trees and other conifers are evergreens.

fiber: a long, thin strand of natural or artificial material. A bird might use it to build a nest.

needles: stiff, pointed leaves, like those of a pine tree.

pigment: a substance in plant or animal tissues that gives them their characteristic color, particularly in autumn.

pounce: to swoop down and grab, like the way an owl catches its prey.

powerful: very strong; having influence.

prolegs: the fleshy legs on the abdomen of an insect larva, such as a caterpillar. The caterpillar uses its prolegs to grip onto twigs.

rascal: a mischievous animal or person.

silent: having no sound; quiet.

silky: soft and smooth, like silk fabric.

stumps: short or broken pieces or parts.

sturdy: strongly built or made.

twigs: the small branches or shoots of a tree or shrub. Some types of birds use twigs for building their nests.

ACTIVITIES

Make a Pinecone Bird Feeder

Make a simple bird feeder with a pinecone. Tie a long piece of string around the cone near its top. Spread peanut butter all over the cone, then roll it in birdseed. Tie the cone to a tree branch and enjoy watching your backyard birds enjoy!

Leave It to You!

Collect autumn leaves in different shapes and colors. Place the leaves between sheets of newspaper. Put a heavy book on top of the newspaper. After the leaves have dried, use them to decorate greeting cards or make a collage.

Leaf Rubbings

Collect different types of leaves and compare the veins and ridges on them. With a pencil and tracing paper, make a rubbing of each leaf.

All Grown Up

Find a book on moths and butterflies in your school or public library. Can you find a picture of the adult luna moth? Think of three words to describe this moth, and then draw its picture.

It Comes from a Tree

Make a list of all the ways that you and your family use products that come from trees, such as nuts, paper, and spices.

Do the Ring Thing!

Count the rings in a tree stump to determine the age of the tree. Are all of the rings (called annual rings) the same size? Can you find some that are thinner, perhaps because there wasn't very much rain that year? While hunting for tree stumps, also look for nests and other animal homes in the trees.

More Books to Read

The Living Tree. Nigel S. Hester (Franklin Watts)

The Nature and Science of Leaves. Exploring the Science of Nature (series).
   Jane Burton and Kim Taylor (Gareth Stevens)

Owls. Animal Families (series). Markus Kappeler (Gareth Stevens)

Raccoon Magic for Kids. Animal Magic for Kids (series). Jeff Fair (Gareth Stevens)

Trees. Young Scientist Concepts and Projects (series). Peter Mellett (Gareth Stevens)

The World of Owls. Where Animals Live (series). David Saintsing (Gareth Stevens)

Videos

I Like Trees. (Video Dimensions)

The Tree: A Living Community. (Churchill Media)

A Tree Is a Living Thing. (Encyclopædia Britannica Educational Corporation)

Web Sites

www.ed.uri.edu/RIProj/facts.html

magic.usi.edu/magic/SS96Web/rainforest/rainforest.html

Some web sites stay current longer than others. For further web sites, use your search engines to locate the following topics: *birds, caterpillars, leaves, owls, raccoons, squirrels,* and *trees.*

INDEX